CW00553745

A FLIGHT TOO

THE STORY OF ELSIE MACKAY
OF GLENAPP

Jack Hunter

Published by
STRANRAER AND DISTRICT LOCAL HISTORY TRUST
Charity No. SCO 28177

For Bill Gill and Paddy O'Neill.

ISBN 978-0-9542966-8-1

© Jack Hunter 2008

Published by
Stranraer and District Local History Trust
Tall Trees
London Road
Stranraer DG9 8BZ

Charity No. SCO 28177

Introduction

Today the name of The Honourable Elsie Mackay of Glenapp is probably not widely recognized either locally or nationally. However eighty years ago Elsie Mackay was a household name constantly in the newspaper columns. This was hardly surprising as she was the daughter of one of the richest and most powerful men in Britain, a wealthy heiress, a leading figure in fashionable London society, a successful stage and screen actress, and a pioneering airwoman. Yet there was another and very different side to Elsie Mackay. In the little world of Glenapp estate in south Ayrshire and in the surrounding villages this glittering, sophisticated, glamorous figure became Miss Elsie, a friendly, sociable, unpretentious person, who cared deeply about local communities and people, particularly those who lived on her father's estate, and who manifested that concern in manifold, unpublicised, practical ways.

Eighty years after the flight which cruelly and prematurely ended her life, it seems appropriate to seek to extend awareness of her remarkable personality and achievements with particular reference to the way in which "Miss Elsie" became the object of such affection and regard in the corner of south-west Scotland she loved so much.

Purists unhappy about the inclusion of Glenapp and its residents in a series of publications supposedly dealing with Wigtownshire should take reassurance from the view of the nineteenth century Ayrshire historian James Paterson. He states that even as late as the eighteenth century Glenapp was considered part of Galloway and relates the old tale of a voyager from Stranraer to Ireland asking a fellow passenger the name of the deep valley running down to Loch Ryan.

The reply was, "That is Glen-App, the wildest glen in a' Galloway and no a bit mair rife wi' dun deer an bonnie nits atween't an the Mull." Who could quibble with that confident assertion?

LIKE FATHER, LIKE DAUGHTER

Elsie Mackay's character and life can be understood only by knowing something about her father as arguably her dominant traits were inherited from him, while a family source confirms the impression gained from the details of her life and the evidence of photographs that she was the favourite of his four daughters and enjoyed a close relationship with her formidable father. And many of the circumstances surrounding her last flight were determined by Lord Inchcape's very prominent and influential position in British public life.

Lord Inchcape and Elsie Mackay on board his yacht *Rover*
Courtesy of Lord and Lady Inchcape

James Lyle Mackay, first Lord Inchcape, was born in Arbroath in 1852, the son of a ship's captain who was also part-owner of two barques trading in the East Indies. His passion for the sea and ships almost brought an untimely end to his career before it had properly started for at the age of eight while on a voyage from Montrose to Archangel in northern Russia he contrived to fall overboard twice, remarkably without ill effects. His father was less fortunate, being drowned when the young Mackay was eleven so that the boy had to seek employment as a clerk with a variety of firms until in 1874 he obtained a post as a general assistant (or perhaps shipping clerk) in Calcutta with the parent company of the British India line. Nineteen years later he returned to Britain as a director of British India, the largest British shipping concern, and was later to become its chairman. In India he had employed his talents to the benefit of the wider community, becoming Sheriff of Calcutta and a member of the Viceroy's Legislative Council.

Back in Britain James Mackay's career continued to flourish. When BI amalgamated with the P&O line in 1914, he became chairman and managing director of both companies and the most powerful man in the British shipping industry. His commitment to public service continued with his abilities being utilized by the government in various capacities for over twenty years. High points were his mission to China in 1901 to negotiate a commercial treaty, his membership of the Imperial Defence Committee during the First World War, and his successful sale in 1921 of the 418 ex-enemy merchant ships allocated to Britain under the Treaty of Versailles. In the last transaction his business acumen earned the government twenty million pounds. More controversial was his membership in 1921-22 of the National Economy Committee, which wielded the infamous "Geddes axe" (so called after the committee chairman), proposing a huge cut of 86 million pounds in government spending. His public service was rewarded successively by a knighthood, a barony, a viscountcy, and finally in 1929, three years before his death, he became Earl of Inchcape, retaining his previous rank in the form of Viscount Glenapp. Along the way he had narrowly missed becoming Viceroy of India and had politely declined the crown of Albania.

THE GLENAPP CONNECTION

Finnarts House in a 1920's postcard
Courtesy of Donnie Nelson

Glenapp Castle in a 1920's postcard. The west and east wings have not yet been added.
Courtesy of Donnie Nelson

The inclusion of "Glenapp" in Lord Inchcape's final title is evidence of his affection for his south Ayrshire property, his favourite residence. Yet he acquired the lands, including Carlock, Auchencrosh, and Smyrton, only in 1917 (for £90,000). They had originally been part of the barony of Ardstinchar, owned for centuries by a branch of the famous Kennedy family. Traditionally the link was created when one Hew Kennedy bought "the ten pund land of Arstensar" in the fifteenth century with the golden handshake he had received from the King of France in recognition of many years' valiant service in that monarch's cause. After the 1816 sale of the barony in fifteen separate lots, most of what is now Glenapp estate passed through several hands, including the Earl of Orkney and an Edinburgh University professor of law, before its acquisition by Inchcape. He extended his holding by purchasing Auchairne and, notably, the small Finnarts estate, the latter giving him possession of the entire glen as well as frontage on Loch Ryan. For some reason James Mackay seems to have wanted to expunge all trace of the previous, Kennedy proprietor of Finnarts. The small mansion house was comprehensively demolished so that today it is difficult to find any trace of it. Only a scattering of pieces of slate, some bricks, and a few fragments of ornamental garden railing betray its location.

Glenapp castle already existed in 1917, having been built in 1870 to the design of David Bryce, architect of Edinburgh's exuberant Fettes College, but its new owner greatly extended it, adding west and east wings. He also made improvements to Carlock House at the head of the glen, which plays an important part in the Elsie Mackay story. Originally a shooting lodge, it had already been upgraded by a previous proprietor. Now it was intended for use by the younger members of the Inchcape family and became a great favourite of his third daughter, Elsie. A more commercial improvement was the construction of the sawmill at Auchencrosh, which still stands beside the A77 nearly opposite the former top entrance to the castle. The extensions to the latter must have been useful for accommodating the guests who arrived in August for the grouse shooting season. The Earl's numerous business connections with India meant that among the visitors for The Twelfth were always several maharajahs and rajahs in their national costume. They arrived by train, the famous Paddy, at Stranraer and were then whisked by limousine to Glenapp. Their presence and attire caused something of a stir among the local residents.

However visiting Eastern potentates were not the only people whose transport needs were catered for at Glenapp. With no bus service between Ayr and Stranraer until the mid-1920s, the Earl had an estate lorry fitted with removable benches down each side. Every second Saturday the vehicle was cleaned and then had the seating installed so that estate workers and their families could spend an afternoon enjoying the attractions of Stranraer.

"THE REAL MACKAY"

 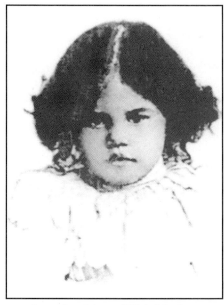

Lady Inchcape
Courtesy of Lord and Lady Inchcape

An early picture of Elsie Mackay
Courtesy of Lord and Lady Inchcape

To this father and into this environment Elsie Mackay, the soon-to-be Sir James Mackay's third of four daughters, was born in 1893. Her mother was the former Jean Shanks. (The Shanks family's connection with Glenapp was to continue until recent years in the persons of the sisters Jean and Marjory Shanks. They lived in the glen in the former manse and were prominent in its community and religious life.) Educated partly at a convent in Belgium, Elsie Mackay, in some ways, conformed to the stereotype that might be anticipated from her background. Gregarious and fond of dancing, she was a leading member of London society.

Elsie Mackay as London society knew her
Courtesy of the late Lord Inchcape

Acting on behalf of her invalid mother, she was a prominent society hostess. As befitted a wealthy heiress who had received one million pounds on her twenty-first birthday in 1914, she was considered one of the best dressed women in the country. She drove a Bentley or Rolls-Royce with head-turning dash and was an expert horsewoman, not just a first-class rider but someone with a gift for handling equines. In 1922 she accompanied her father on the maiden return voyage of the White Star liner *Majestic* from Southampton to New York; in 1923 she launched the P & O liner *Maloja*. James Mackay purchased the Park-Dunragit estate near Stranraer reputedly for Elsie and in the hope that she might be attracted to the life of a country lady.

"Poppy Wyndham" in a studio
publicity photo

If this was the case, his hopes were disappointed. The age of female emancipation had dawned and his third daughter was an enthusiastic believer. During the First World War her mother opened her own hospital for wounded soldiers and, despite her lack of knowledge of nursing, Elsie Mackay insisted on becoming heavily involved. This involvement led to a second display of emancipation when she fell in love with one of the patients, South African actor Dennis Wyndham, who had been wounded while fighting with the Wiltshire regiment.

In spite of parental disapproval and the consequent threat of disinheritance, the couple eloped to Glasgow and were married there. In all this Elsie displayed the paternal determination, strength of character, independence, adventurousness, and willingness to take risks. The annulment of the marriage in 1922 was another demonstration of those traits.

However, the marriage had one lasting legacy. Prior to the outbreak of the Great War Elsie had displayed her emancipation credentials by opting for a stage career, becoming at the age of twenty the youngest leading lady in London's West End in the play *Grumpy*. She adopted, presumably after marriage, the stage name of Poppy Wyndham and retained it when she moved into the world of films, again with considerable success. Between 1919 and 1921 she appeared in at least eight productions, admittedly in supporting roles but twice in notable company, that of Ronald Colman in *A Son of David* and *Snow in the Desert*. In *The Great Coup* she had the opportunity to display her riding skills. It would be tempting to suggest that the Elsie Mackay who appeared in two Broadway plays was the lady from Glenapp but it would also be irresponsible: it does not appear that at this stage of her career she acted under her own name, which was shared by a contemporary American actress.

"Poppy Wyndham" in *The Great Coup*
Courtesy of Historic Newspapers

In her stage and film career the Honourable Elsie displayed qualities complementary to and very different from those inherited from her father. In spite of the gulf in backgrounds she established excellent relations with the supporting actresses and extras with whom she worked. She exhibited no traces of superiority and expected no special treatment. Her natural, vivacious, unaffected manner together with her kindness and generosity made her very popular and led to her receiving the nickname "The Real Mackay". Her appearance was as attractive as her personality: she was slim and petite with strikingly beautiful brown eyes and jet black, wavy hair of which she was so proud that for long she refused to bob it in the contemporary fashion.

The dress of the boy in the background suggests this photo. of Elsie Mackay may have been taken on a film set

The qualities that made her the object of such affection backstage and on film sets had exactly the same effect on the residents of her father's Glenapp estate and the surrounding area. She spent as much time there as a busy life permitted, becoming after her siblings' marriages the mistress of Carlock House at the head of the glen. From there with characteristic energy she involved herself in the life of the estate and the parish. In the words of a local resident of the period,

"She looked after Ballantrae."

For the children she organized Christmas parties with lavish presents and outings, which she led, to cinemas and other attractions. For adults she arranged concerts followed by dances in Ballantrae public hall to raise funds for some local good cause as well as functions for estate workers. In all those activities she participated fully, often having driven up from London overnight, even in winter, to finalize preparations. But much of the good she did was done informally and unobtrusively. She was a regular visitor at the homes of the elderly and the sick on the estate, on one occasion paying for a necessary but otherwise unaffordable operation. In its obituary of her the local newspaper quoted the instance of an apprentice gardener on the estate who had completed his apprenticeship and was moving to a new appointment. Elsie Mackay personally gave him a sum of money and a wrist watch before sending him to the station in her own car.

And her activities extended beyond the estate and Ballantrae parish. Just seven months before her death and newly returned from Poland she provided the entertainment at the monthly meeting of the Cairnryan WRI, singing four Scots songs. Her death prevented her being the main attraction at Stranraer aquatic sports in July, 1928. Characteristically she had promised "her wholehearted assistance", offering to give a flying exhibition above the harbour before taking passengers on flights by seaplane to Cairnryan and back. For this purpose she was going to take lessons in flying a seaplane and then hire one for the occasion. Money raised by the Cairnryan trips was to go to the sports' funds.

A CAREER CHANGE

While the local area enjoyed the benefits of her company, enthusiasm, and generosity right to the end of her life, the sorority of London stage and film actresses was less fortunate. In 1922, the year her marriage ended, she embarked on a career change and became deeply involved with her father's P&O company. A contemporary source credits her with marine engineering expertise, and she may well have been active on the business side, but her energies were mainly channelled into interior design. She was responsible for the decoration of some of the suites and public rooms of no less than twelve P&O liners. It is easy to conclude that she obtained those commissions through a father's indulgence towards his favourite daughter but Lord Inchcape was famously a hard-headed business man and would not have entrusted his top-of-the-range suites and first-class accommodation to someone whose professionalism was in any doubt.

In fact his daughter's bold and stylish designs were hugely successful. A notable achievement was the *Cathay* with its green, Jacobean smoke room and its Adam music room but her greatest triumph came with the *Viceroy of India*, the company's most successful ship of its generation, offering new levels of splendour and comfort. Elsie Mackay's designs here entered the world of fantasy. The First-Class smoking room was like the great hall of a castle with hammer beams, crossed swords on the walls, a huge fireplace surmounted by a coat of arms, and appropriately period furniture. Equally eye-catching were the music room in eighteenth century style; the dining room with its blue, marbled pillars; the reading room again in the Adam mode (perhaps the Scottish connection appealed); and the company's first indoor swimming pool complete with wall decorations evocative of the Roman city of Pompeii. Purists might have blanched but the well-to-do travelling public loved it. Sadly the designer did not live to enjoy her success for the *Viceroy* was launched the year after her death.

The First-Class smoking room on the *Viceroy of India*
Courtesy of P&O.

The swimming pool on the *Viceroy of India*
Courtesy of P&O

1922 was a profoundly significant year for Elsie Mackay as she also found a second outlet for her energy and ambition, one which bulked even larger in her life than interior design and was to lead to her death. Undeterred by an incident on a scheduled London-Paris flight, when her plane lost part of its rudder in a gale, she became a convert to the infant form of travel, flying. Perhaps the rudder incident appealed to her sense of adventure and fearlessness. She learned to fly at Hendon with one of the great names of early aviation, Sir Alan Cobham, bought a de Havilland DH 6 plane, and obtained her pilot's licence. A flippant comment in a London newspaper that the Honourable Elsie was setting a fashionable style was very far wide of the mark for flying to her was an extremely serious business. Again perhaps displaying her similarities to her father, she was interested in its commercial possibilities as a time-saving way to travel. She established a reputation as a steady, serious pilot and gained a knowledge of aircraft construction and aero engines. These achievements led to her appointment in 1925 as the only woman on the Advisory Committee of Pilots to the Air League.

Elsie Mackay in flying kit
Courtesy of Historic Newspapers

"I DO NOT INTEND TO COMMIT SUICIDE"

However, the lure of record-breaking flight attempts, initially ignored, was to prove an irresistible and fatal attraction to some sides of Elsie Mackay's personality. A friend believed that the seeds of what became her consuming double ambition to make the first east-west crossing of the Atlantic by plane and the first either way by a woman were sown in the summer of 1927. The occasion was a triumphal visit to London by the American Charles Lindbergh, first person to make a solo, non-stop flight by plane across the Atlantic. Whether this view is true or not, it was soon after that Elsie began to make preparations for a record attempt, well aware of the danger involved: in the previous seven months seven fliers, including two women, had died attempting the east-west crossing. She faced two sets of obstacles, one geographical and one human.

The geographical obstacles were twofold, firstly the sheer distance (a minimum of 2,000 miles, entirely over water) and secondly the fact that the east-west crossing against the prevailing winds is much more difficult than that from west to east. Modern trans-Atlantic holidaymakers know the difference that wind direction makes to the times of the respective flights. Elsie Mackay realised she needed the best possible assistance to meet those challenges. Well aware that a solo flight was not a realistic option (earlier unsuccessful attempts had involved crews of three and four) she sought a top-class pilot to accompany her. After an unsuccessful approach to an ex-RAF pilot friend, whose war injuries ruled out long flights, she sought the assistance of acquaintances in the Air Ministry and was directed to one Captain W.G.R. Hinchliffe.

Captain Hinchliffe's credentials were, to say the least, impressive. A natural pilot of remarkable ability with a distinguished war record (apart from some non-operational problems) and a DFC, he was also a vastly experienced commercial flier. He had been the first chief pilot of Dutch airline KLM before transferring to Britain's Imperial Airways. By 1927 he had amassed nearly 9,000 hours of flying time while his commercial experience had made him an experienced navigator, meteorologist, and bad weather flier. He was also likely to be amenable to a realistic business proposition. He had lost his left eye in a wartime flying accident, his remaining eye was giving problems, and he realised new health and fitness regulations might end his flying career. His financial affairs were in a poor shape (a recurring problem since his RAF days), and he had a wife and two young children to support.

Captn W.G.R. Hinchliffe
Courtesy of Historic Newspapers

A meeting between the potential team proved mutually satisfactory. It was agreed that Hinchliffe would attempt the east-west crossing of the Atlantic with Elsie as second pilot. In return he would receive a salary of eighty pounds monthly plus expenses, collect all the substantial prize monies on offer for a successful flight, and have a life insurance for £10,000 taken out on his behalf. He would also choose and equip the plane for the attempt. It is easy to conclude that he was influenced by the Mackay charm and wealth but it seems just as likely that he was impressed by her reputation as a highly competent, experienced pilot with considerable professional, aeronautical knowledge. For his part, he too went about his business very professionally. Deciding that no British-manufactured plane met his requirements, he went to the United

States and purchased a Stinson Detroiter, single-engined monoplane, a well tried type in extensive commercial use there. The cockpit had dual controls and a heater while the cabin was roomy, providing accommodation for seven passengers. The Wright Whirlwind engine had proved its reliability and been used by Lindbergh. Its top speed with a light load was 130mph.

Hinchliffe made the preparations with meticulous care. He had once retorted to someone urging him to speed up preparations for a flight,
"I do not intend to commit suicide,"
and no detail was overlooked or unchecked. The Stinson was shipped over to Britain in sections and reassembled at Brooklands airfield under Hinchliffe's personal supervision. A mechanic was brought across from the Wright company to ensure that the engine was expertly attended to. Maps and weather charts were pored over to determine the best possible route. The question of fuel supply was given particular attention. The minimum distance to be covered was 2,300 miles from RAF Cranwell to Newfoundland but the more desirable destination of New York took the distance up to 3,300 miles with the tempting possibility of a final leg to Philadelphia to claim a £5,000 prize. Careful calculations, checked and rechecked, led Hinchliffe to conclude that with two people on board the Stinson's modest 200hp engine could lift 480 gallons of fuel into the air, more than Lindbergh had carried, and thus obtain approximately 45 hours flying time and a range of over 4,000 miles. The safety margin built in proved the truth of Hinchliffe's "suicide" comment. To achieve this fuel capacity the plane's wing tanks had to be augmented by a 225-gallon tank installed in the cabin in place of the passenger seats and seventeen specially made aluminium petrol cans, the aluminium saving a few, extra, precious pounds of weight.

But why start at RAF Cranwell on the east side of the country and thus add significantly to the distance to be covered? The answer was that Cranwell runway, over a mile long, was the only one in Britain that would give the heavily laden Stinson enough distance to become airborne. However, the solution merely created another obstacle, for the RAF, mindful of the growing criticism of east-west flight attempts after the heavy casualty rate, refused permission for the airfield's use. Here the second pilot's networking skills came into play and a direct approach by Elsie to the air minister, an acquaintance, yielded permission for the use of Cranwell for one week only. With the addition to the aircraft of extra equipment to aid navigation, it seemed that everything possible was being done to counter the natural obstacles to the flight.

That left the human obstacles, concentrated in the person of Elsie's formidable father, Lord Inchcape. His fondness for his favourite daughter ensured that the planned flight would meet his total opposition; his power and influence meant that his opposition was likely to be insurmountable. The strategy adopted to circumvent the problem was twofold. Firstly, every effort would be made to ensure his lordship knew nothing of the record attempt. To this end everyone involved was sworn to secrecy and a press blackout was attempted. But even in 1928 in a less intrusive media age this seemed unlikely to succeed and so an additional plan was prepared. The aid of a friend of Hinchliffe, a former RAF pilot called Gordon Sinclair, was enlisted. If news of the flight leaked out, then Sinclair would be identified as the second pilot with Elsie Mackay in the role of financial backer and nothing more. (In fact, a remark the lady reportedly made to a close friend indicated that initially her plan might have been for three pilots, with Sinclair the third, but that he was sacrificed in favour of additional fuel.)

Captn Gordon Sinclair
Courtesy of Historic Newspapers

THE EVE OF BATTLE

It was RAF Cranwell and the neighbouring village of Leadham in Lincolnshire that became the focus of the unfolding drama at the end of February, 1928. It was thither that on the 24th Hinchliffe brought the Stinson Detroiter monoplane resplendent in its livery of black with the wings and struts picked out in gold, the colour scheme perhaps the last creation of Elsie Mackay's interior design career. It carried its name *Endeavour* on the front of the fuselage; at Cranwell patriotic RAF mechanics painted Union Jacks on each side of the rear fuselage. The aircraft had been and continued to be extensively test flown by Hinchliffe and Mackay, the latter claiming she had been on every flight. Her handling of the plane, including a solo stint, had earned the approval of Hinchliffe, who described her to his wife as "a rattling good pilot". The senior pilot stayed at the venerable George Hotel in Leadham a mile from the airfield while Elsie Mackay commuted from London. The George became the project's unofficial headquarters. There too stayed Gordon Sinclair, who, by his own account, had accompanied his friend to Cranwell and remained for the duration of the expedition's stay. An excellent mechanic, he helped to prepare the Stinson monoplane for the flight.

The George Hotel, Leadham, today
Courtesy of the George Hotel

To Cranwell and indeed a large part of eastern England came also a very unwelcome arrival, a spell of severe weather which laid Lincolnshire under a blanket of snow and made a postponement of the flight inevitable. This caused major problems because the permitted week at Cranwell expired and pressure was applied to Hinchliffe to move out. In addition he could feel rivals breathing down his neck, almost certainly not the twelve teams he quoted to a reporter but definitely a German crew, whose preparations were well advanced. But perhaps the biggest problem was created by another unwelcome visitor. For the first line of defence against Lord Inchcape's learning of the attempt had failed: the story had been leaked to the *Daily Express*, which on 8th March not only announced the imminent flight but claimed that Elsie Mackay would be second pilot. Although Lord Inchcape was abroad in Egypt with his ailing wife, his long arm ensured a speedy response. A heavyweight Inchcape team promptly appeared on the scene. It consisted of Elsie's only brother and the Hon. Alexander Shaw, husband of her eldest sister, Margaret, and later chairman of the P&O line in succession to his father-in-law.

What was said at their meeting with Elsie will never be known but two days after the flight started Margaret Shaw was quoted in a newspaper as saying that her sister had definitely promised not to go. If the report is correct, it means that the would-be record breaker broke her promise to her family, something which seems highly unlikely in view of all that is known about her: when she defied her father, as she sometimes did, she had the strength of character to do so openly and frankly. Perhaps a communication breakdown occurred and Elsie had merely promised to review her decision to take part in the flight, duly and carefully doing so without changing her mind.

All these circumstances created huge pressure to attempt the flight as soon as possible and on Monday, the twelfth of March, with the weather improving, Hinchliffe apparently told his mechanics that the duo would depart early next day. Decoy Gordon Sinclair was already on site; the pretence that he was second pilot was to be maintained right up to a few minutes before take-off. To Leadham and the George Hotel came Elsie Mackay and a friend Ms de Pries, each in a chauffeur-driven limousine and accompanied by a maid. Ms de Pries signed the register for both.

After dinner that evening Hinchliffe returned to the airfield to supervise final preparations. Elsie, a convert to the Roman Catholic faith, attended confession at the local church and then returned to the hotel. There, presumably through the agency of room service, she ordered quantities of sandwiches and fruit together with flasks of coffee and soup as provisions for the flight.

One of the difficulties in establishing what happened in the last few hours at Leadham and Cranwell is that the contemporary newspaper reports differ on essential details, a circumstance not unfamiliar to the modern reader. And so it was either at four o'clock or five (more probably the latter) in the morning that the principals were called by hotel staff and shortly afterwards set off in two limousines for Cranwell. On the way Elsie Mackay stopped at the RC church and by prior arrangement took communion with the local priest, Father Arenzen. She told him she was going on a journey across the Atlantic, impressed on him the need for secrecy, and promised to send a cable on her arrival. He later described her state as excited but emotional. Her concern about secrecy surely suggests she had not promised the Inchcape family to withdraw from the flight. If she had given such a promise, secrecy was unnecessary for the family would have been lulled into a false sense of security and consequent inactivity.

Accounts of events at Cranwell lack unanimity. One version has Sinclair taking his place in the plane while final preparations were made, emerging at the last possible moment to be replaced by Elsie. Another version has only her entering the plane but so muffled in her flying suit as to be unrecognizable. However the existence of a photograph of Elsie and Hinchliffe posing beside the Stinson in the last minutes before it took off indicates that at the very last the pretence was discarded for the handful of RAF personnel and two chauffeurs watching. Hinchliffe, although the lead pilot, climbed as was his wont into the right-hand, co-pilot's seat for this gave his remaining eye its maximum field of vision. At 8.35 on Tuesday, the thirteenth of March, the heavily-laden Stinson, virtually a flying petrol tanker, trundled down the frozen carpet of snow on the grass runway for what must have seemed an interminable mile before struggling into the unwelcoming sky. The die was cast.

The crew of *Endeavour* photographed a few minutes before take-off

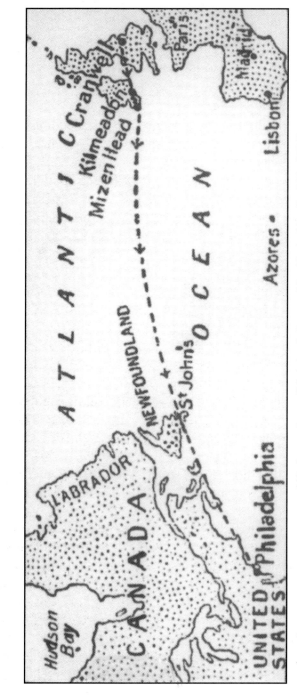

A contemporary newspaper map of *Endeavour*'s possible intended route. New York, 90 miles NE of Philadelphia, is not shown
Courtesy of Lord and Lady Inchcape

"OUR FRIEND LEFT AT 8.35"

The first news that the record attempt was under way came in a cable from Cranwell (sent by Gordon Sinclair?) to Captain Hinchliffe's agent (surely a modern touch) in New York,

"Our friend left at 8.35".

A message to a London newspaper confirmed the tidings less tersely. The news spread rapidly on both sides of the Atlantic for its major intrinsic interest was heightened by two fascinating questions, the identity of the second pilot and the aircraft's destination. Clearly not everyone read and believed the *Daily Express* for, despite its March 8th report, newspaper headlines the day after the start of the flight declared "Passenger Mystery Deepens" and "Passenger's Identity Puzzle" while an alleged eyewitness of the Cranwell departure categorically stated in the *Glasgow Herald*,

"The passenger in the machine was Mr Gordon Sinclair." Harry Lloyd, Hinchliffe's English (*sic*) agent stirred the pot by suggesting that all three parties were in the Stinson. The mystery remained unsolved until the Wednesday evening, 36 hours after the plane's departure, when, as he had been instructed, Gordon Sinclair appeared from hiding to confirm that the *Endeavour*'s second pilot was the Hon. Elsie Mackay. The reason for maintaining the deception long after the need to keep Lord Inchcape at arm's length was apparently commercial. It was felt that the publicity gained by a successful conclusion to the flight would be enhanced when the co-pilot was dramatically revealed not as a former RAF officer but a glamorous heiress.

The second question had been posed by Hinchliffe himself. Presumably to confuse possible rivals, he dropped hints that his destination was India and a non-stop flight record. The day before his departure from Cranwell he told a reporter that he had not yet decided whether to go to America or India. Had his claim been true, it would surely have represented the ultimate in traveller destination-vacillation. But this question was answered before the previous one. Three hours after *Endeavour*'s departure, Civic Guards in Kilmeaden in County Waterford relayed a message reporting an aircraft flying high and fast in a westerly direction at 11.30 a.m. in heavy snow and poor visibility. Hinchliffe's target was America.

On that side of the Atlantic excitement rose. As the hour of possible landfall neared on Wednesday morning, the sealing fleet 150 miles north-east of Newfoundland was urged to scan the skies for *Endeavour*; reports of sightings of lone planes over Newfoundland and the New England states proliferated; crowds descended on New York's Mitchell Field to welcome the aviators; and extra police were drafted to the aerodrome at Philadelphia to ensure a possible arrival there was an orderly one. Sadly the crowds gathered and the police were mobilized in vain for the multitude of reports of single planes seen and heard in eastern American skies all proved false. After Waterford the only genuine sightings of the Stinson came on the same day and on the same side of the Atlantic as the Civic Guards' report.

A second sighting, this time at Kinsale, tracked Hinchliffe and Mackay along Ireland's south coast to Mizen Head in County Cork. There the lighthouse keepers, endorsed by the Crookshaven coastguard and local residents, reported a plane passing over at 1.30 p.m. flying low and fast in poor conditions of sleet and snow. With a headwind to contend with, it headed out into the grey wastes of the Atlantic, which stretched forbiddingly ahead for nearly two thousand miles. The heavily laden aircraft had averaged 80mph over the first leg of the flight. Thereafter the only time the black-and-gold Stinson was ever seen again was by a steamer 170 miles off the coast of Ireland. Its report was of a large plane flying low overhead in a westerly direction. Messages from other ships were ominous. While the weather on both seaboards was relatively innocuous, the mid-Atlantic was in the grip of a severe storm.

As the winds raged, hope reluctantly died. By midday on Thursday, the fifteenth, over fifty hours after take-off, it was impossible that *Endeavour* could still be in the air as her fuel would have been exhausted. Two faint glimmers of light remained. The plane could have landed in a remote, wooded part of Newfoundland, New England, or even Canada, leaving the occupants struggling to reach civilization. The passage of time extinguished that possibility. The final refuge for the optimist was the chance that the stricken aircraft had ditched at sea providentially close to a passing ship and been rescued but that without wireless the vessel could not transmit the good news. Improbable as this might seem in the vastness of the Atlantic, it had actually happened to two previous aircrews on record attempts. But this time no vessel berthed with grateful survivors and as the days went by the cruel fact had to be acknowledged. Human courage and skill had challenged the Atlantic … and lost. Glenapp would not see "Miss Elsie" again.

AFTERMATH

Even after the failure of the Hinchliffe - Mackay record attempt had become an inescapable fact, the flight continued to dominate the newspapers because of its high-profile participants. A media-fuelled campaign to impose legal restrictions on similar enterprises met with lukewarm reaction from the aviation celebrities canvassed and was soon abandoned. More prolonged was the furore over the very real financial plight of Dutch-born Mrs Hinchliffe and her two daughters, one aged four-and-a-half years and the other only three months. Her husband had sought to ensure that however the record attempt ended his family's financial future was secure. However his widow discovered to her consternation that a major problem existed with the £10,000 life insurance policy taken out on his behalf by Elsie Mackay shortly before the departure from Cranwell. The paperwork had been duly done and a cheque handed over for the single premium of £2,700. However, in a situation perhaps not unknown to readers, Elsie had omitted to ensure that her current account held sufficient funds to honour the cheque. It was an understandable oversight in the flurry of final preparations but a disastrous one for the policy had consequently never come into force and no payout could be made.

Theoretically no problem needed to exist because Elsie Mackay's estate of over £600,000 before death duties could obviously make good the omission. However Lord Inchcape, the trustee, had ambitious plans to use the money to commemorate his daughter in a way typical of his career-long commitment to his country. He proposed to invest it in its entirety long-term but for not more than fifty years so that eventually the accumulated total could be used to reduce the National Debt. The press was not impressed, the clamour continued, and questions were asked in parliament, where Chancellor Winston Churchill pointed out that the government had no involvement in the matter. Lord Inchcape then resolved the issue with a personal donation of £10,000 to a fund "for the benefit of sufferers from the Atlantic flight disaster of March last", effectively Mrs Hinchliffe and her daughters.

His impersonal approach may stem from a claim made by Elsie's eldest sister to a reporter not long after *Endeavour*'s departure that Hinchliffe had promised a member of the Inchcape family that he would not take Elsie Mackay with him. It is difficult to see how the pilot could realistically have given such an undertaking when the lady owned the plane and was his employer.

The Hinchliffe family's financial security, then, was ensured. But the widow was not yet to escape the headlines. For in the aftermath of the Great War and its countless bereavements without farewells this was the heyday of spiritualism. In April, perhaps inevitably, Emilie Hinchliffe was approached by a medium who claimed to have had communication with her dead husband. With the encouragement of famous author Sir Arthur Conan Doyle a séance was arranged and extra-terrestrial communication effected. This provided a graphic description of the flight's last hours. Allegedly the plane had suffered severe structural damage from a ferocious storm compounded by multiple mechanical problems. Hinchliffe had turned south to seek the sanctuary of the Azores but had been forced to land the crippled aircraft in the sea well short of his destination. The fliers had lapsed into unconsciousness and met a peaceful end.

Those unconvinced of the efficacy of the spiritualist approach had to wait until December of the same year for evidence of the flight's conclusion. In that month part of an aircraft undercarriage was washed ashore in County Donegal. A wheel bore the manufacturer's name, the Goodrich Company of Ohio, and a reference number. This information allowed a certain identification of the wreckage as having come from *Endeavour*. Whether the location of the find meant that Hinchliffe had turned back because of bad weather, it is impossible to tell. By a strange coincidence the Goodrich Company today has a facility at Prestwick airport barely forty miles from Glenapp.

But the story of the ill-fated flight offers another extra-terrestrial element for as a direct result Leadham's George Hotel reputedly gained a long-term, regular visitor. According to local tradition, March twilights bring the opportunity to glimpse a tall but insubstantial figure, clad in a flying suit and sporting an eye patch, stride noiselessly across the yard. . . .

A less contentious and more corporeal link with the events of March, 1928, is provided by the hotel's present proprietor. When he came to the George nearly 40 years ago, the staff included an elderly local man who had spent his entire working life at the establishment. Len King well remembered the crew of the *Endeavour*'s stay and talked frequently about those momentous days.

FOOTPRINTS IN THE SANDS OF TIME

Lord and Lady Inchcape's altruistic and patriotic grand design to commemorate their lost daughter duly resulted in the creation of the Elsie Mackay Fund, whereby just over £500,000 was invested in government and local authority stocks for approximately fifty years. In 1977 the stocks realized an impressive five million pounds, ten times the original investment. Sadly the National Debt had also increased and at an even greater rate so that it was forty times larger than in 1928: Lord Inchcape, a byword for economical financial management in his business affairs, would have been unimpressed.

Smaller-scale forms of commemoration focused on tiny Glenapp church nestling on the green valley floor halfway down the glen.

Glenapp church in a 1930's postcard   *Courtesy of Donnie Nelson*

The Inchcape parents received approval to create a memorial for their third daughter inside the church. Its centrepiece is a three-light, stained glass window in the east gable depicting Jesus risen and crowned in glory. The right panel contains a likeness of Elsie Mackay. The church was also extensively renovated with the woodwork replaced in oak. Noteworthy details include a pulpit fall with a Celtic design embroidered at the Royal School of Art Needlework in Kensington and the Celtic and Pictish symbols carved on the oak bases of the wall lamps. But for many people the memorial that catches the imagination lies outside the church on the lower slopes of the hillside on the other side of the road. Here the bereaved parents planted a group of rhododendrons (supplied by the Stranraer firm of Thomas Smith) laid out to spell "Elsie". Time has blurred the outlines of the letters but with a little effort and imagination the word can still be discerned, especially in early summer when the rhododendrons are in bloom.

Dedication of Elsie Mackay memorial window in Glenapp church: Lord Inchcape (facing camera) and Lord Stair (in top hat)
Courtesy of Lord and Lady Inchcape

The Elsie Mackay memorial window in Glenapp church. Elsie Mackay is portrayed in the right-hand light.
The dedication reads— To the glory of God in remembrance of the Hon. Elsie Mackay who died 13th March, 1928
© The author

The memorial pulpit fall in Glenapp church
© The author

The Pictish "swimming elephant" motif on a wall lamp base in Glenapp church
© The author

No less effective a memorial took a less tangible form. Soon after the ill-fated flight an elegiac poem was composed by a local author, Gibb Pitt. It circulated and proved so popular that copies were printed. Framed versions hung in many houses in the glen and on the estate, in at least one case for sixty years. Even today, eight decades on, the poem's eloquent simplicity and quiet grief are deeply moving. Elsie Mackay, mistress of Carlock House, could surely have wished for no more sincere or appropriate epitaph:

Grey are the skies abune Glenapp,
And wae is ilka hert.
The vera birds hae quat their sang
And dule lies every airt.
By prood Carlock and Beneraird,
Roun ilka hearth and hame,
Baith young and auld wi tearfu ee
Fu saftly speak her name.
Hers was the lichtsome loyal hert,
The glint o joy atween;
The weary cottars' welcome cheer,
The bairnies' Fairy Queen.
Nae mair, alas, the lichted ha,
Nae mair sic nichts o glee;
Nae mair the hert we loed sae weel,
Oh, cruel, cruel sea.
And when the holly decks the ha
On merry Christmas Day,
Think kindly, oh, think kindly then
O her that made it sae.

(abridged)

ACKNOWLEDGEMENTS

Much of the material in this book is the result of painstaking research by the late Bill Gill and the late Paddy O'Neill, both of whom were greatly interested in the Elsie Mackay story. Douglas Brown generously made available the information he has obtained, particularly about her career as an actress. Lord and Lady Inchcape gave me access to the family archive of newspaper cuttings. These furnished important details not given in later accounts and gave a sense of immediacy, turning history into the here and now. Over the years many local people have contributed personal or family memories to Bill, Paddy, or me; mindful of the sin of omission, I take refuge in a collective acknowledgement. Mae and Donnie Nelson provided invaluable help with the illustrations. Irene Heron prepared the text with her usual professionalism. Alan Hall gave practical encouragement, while Captain Val Plant greatly facilitated copyright clearance. To all those people I am deeply indebted and grateful. Nevertheless, all factual errors, conclusions, speculations, and assumptions are my sole responsibility.

Every effort has been made to trace and acknowledge copyright ownership of the illustrations. Where this has been unsuccessful, relevant information for inclusion in a subsequent edition would be welcomed.

BIBLIOGRAPHY

Anon.	*Glenapp Parish Church*	n.d.
Barker, Ralph	*Great Mysteries of the Air*	London, 1966
Borland, J. McI.	*Ballantrae*	privately pbd.1931
Fuller, John G.	*The Airmen Who Would Not Die*	London, 1981
Howarth, David	*The Story of P&O*	London, 1986
McColm, Jas	*A Time to Remember*	unpbd MS n.d.
McGregor, W.	*Glenapp Parish Church*	n.d.
Pitt, Nick	*Gone with the Wind —*	
	The *Sunday Times Magazine*,	June 2, 2002

The *Daily Express*	various issues of March, 1928
The *Daily Mirror*	various issues of March, 1928
The *Evening Standard*	various issues of March, 1928
The *Glasgow Herald*	various issues of March and August, 1928
The *New York Times*	issue of May 20th, 1922
The *Scotsman*	various issues of March, 1928
The *Sunday Express*	issue of May 18th, 1977
The *Times*	various issues of March, 1928
The *Wigtownshire Free Press*	various issues of November, 1917; August, 1927; March and April, 1928; May, 1932

Previous Trust Publications

Stranraer in World War Two	— Archie Bell
The Loss of the PrincessVictoria	— Jack Hunter
The Cairnryan Military Railway *	— Bill Gill
A Peep at Stranraer's Past	— Donnie Nelson
Royal Burgh of Stranraer 1617 —2000	— J.S. Boyd
	— Jack Hunter
	— Donnie Nelson
	— Christine Wilson
Don't Plague the Ferryman *	— Trevor Boult
Portpatrick to Donaghadee *	— Fraser G. MacHaffie
The Rhinns Forgotten Air Disaster *	— Sandy Rankin
Place-names in the Rhinns of Galloway	— Prof. John MacQueen
Auld Lang Syne in the Rhins of Galloway	— Prof. Charles McNeil
The Lost Town of Innermessan	— Jack Hunter
Every Beach a Port	— Bill McCormack
Aircrew in Wartime	— Norman Fidler
Prehistoric Settlement in the Wigtownshire Moors	— Dr. Jane Murray
100 Years of Stranraer Golf Club	— James Blair, Andrew Hannay and James Sproule
Garlieston —Emergence of a Village	— David Kirkwood

* Out of Print.

Stranraer and District Local History Trust
Membership 2008

Mrs Sheelagh Afia
Mr Peter Armitage
Mrs Elaine Barton
Mr Archie Bell, *Vice-Chairman*
Mrs Dorothy Bell
Mr Douglas Brown
Mrs H. G. Brown
Mr David B. Cairns
Mr John Cameron
Mrs Pat Cameron
Mr John Carruth
Mrs Harriet Collins
Mrs Marion Cunningham
Mr J. P. Davis
Lord Dervaird
Mr Bill Dougan
Mr Jim Ferguson
Mr Norman Fidler
Mr C. J. Findlay
Miss Dora Gorman
Mrs Irene Grant
Mr Tom Hargreaves
Mrs A. C. Harkness
Mr John Harkness
Mrs M. J. Heaney
Mr W. A. Heaney
Mr Richard Holme
Mr Peter Holmes
Mr Jack Hunter
Mr David Kirkwood
Mr P. H. K. Lilley
Mr Robert Lindsay
Mrs Margaret MacArthur
Mrs Rosemary McCormack
Mr Colin McCubbin
Dr Christine McDowell
Mrs Irene McKie

Mrs Nancy McLucas
Prof. John MacQueen
Mrs Winifred MacQueen
Mrs Margaret Matthews
Mr Harry Monteith
Dr Jane Murray
Mr Alasdair Morgan
Mrs Lynn Neild
Mr Donnie Nelson, MBE, *Chairman*
Mrs Mae Nelson
Mrs Helen Nish
Mr Wolf Richthofen
Mr John Pickin
Mr Jim Pratt
Mrs Margaret Pratt
Mr Jim Rafferty
Mrs Helen Scott
Mr J. D. Sharp
Mr P. N. Skinner
Dr E. A. W. Slater
Mrs Renee Smith
Lady Stair
Mr Bill Stanley
Mr D. J. Start
Mrs Sheila Stevenson
Mr Tom Stevenson, *Treasurer*
Mr Russell Walker
Mr Owen Watt
Mr David Williamson
Mr David Willison
Mrs Christine Wilson, *Secretary*
Mrs Elizabeth Wilson
Mr Eric Wilson
Mr William Wilson
Stranraer & District Chamber of Commerce

Stranraer and District Local History Trust was constituted in 1998 at the instigation of Stranraer and District Chamber of Commerce.

National News Service